LOW-BEGINNING

Health Stories

Readings and Language Activities
for Healthy Choices

D0506497

Ann Gianola

Instructor, San Diego Community College District
Instructor, University of San Diego English Language Academy
San Diego, California

New Readers Press

Health Stories: Readings and Language Activities for Healthy Choices
Low Beginning
ISBN 978-1-56420-701-2

Copyright © 2007 New Readers Press
New Readers Press
ProLiteracy's Publishing Division
1320 Jamesville Avenue, Syracuse, New York 13210
www.newreaderspress.com

Printed in the United States of America
9 8 7 6 5 4

Proceeds from the sale of New Readers Press materials support professional
development, training, and technical assistance programs of ProLiteracy
that benefit local literacy programs in the U.S. and around the globe.

Developmental Editor: Paula L. Schlusberg
Creative Director: Andrea Woodbury
Illustrations: George Hamblin, Seitu Hayden and Roger Audette, Represented by Wilkinson Studios Inc.
Production Specialist: Maryellen Casey

Contents

LESSON 1

Choosing Juice

Zahra is at the supermarket. She is with her daughter, Lela. Zahra is looking for orange juice. Her family drinks orange juice every morning. Zahra finds the juices in aisle four. Lela points to a big orange bottle. "Let's buy that one, Mom. It's delicious. I drink it at my friend's house."

Zahra picks up the bottle. Then she looks at the **Nutrition Facts** label. This orange juice has many **ingredients.** It has water and a lot of sugar. It has only 10% orange juice. Then there is a long list of **chemicals.** There is also **dye** for color. Zahra doesn't want her family to drink it.

Zahra puts down the bottle. "Sorry," she says. "I'm not buying that one. It isn't very **healthy.**" Zahra picks up another bottle. She reads the label. It says 100% orange juice. She puts it in her shopping cart. "Okay," says Zahra. "Now we need milk."

"Let's buy the pink, strawberry-flavored milk," says Lela. "It's delicious. I drink it at my friend's house."

Check *Yes* or *No.*

Yes   No

____ ____   1. Zahra and Lela are at the supermarket.

____ ____   2. Zahra is looking for pink, strawberry-flavored milk.

____ ____   3. Her family drinks orange juice once a week.

____ ____   4. Lela points to a big orange bottle in aisle four.

____ ____   5. Zahra looks at the Nutrition Facts label.

____ ____   6. This orange juice has 90% fruit juice.

____ ____   7. It has a long list of chemicals and dye for color.

____ ____   8. Zahra wants her family to drink it.

____ ____   9. Zahra picks up a bottle that has 100% orange juice.

____ ____   10. Lela drinks 100% orange juice at her friend's house.

Complete each sentence.

bottle	dye	juice	shopping cart
chemicals	family	label	supermarket

1. Zahra and her daughter are at the _____.

2. Lela points to a big orange _____.

3. Zahra looks at the Nutrition Facts _____.

4. This orange _____ has many ingredients.

5. It has a long list of _____.

6. There is also _____ for color.

7. Zahra doesn't want her _____ to drink it.

8. She puts 100% juice in her _____.

Matching: Opposites

____ 1. healthy   a. small

____ 2. picks up   b. night

____ 3. delicious   c. tasteless

____ 4. morning   d. bad for you

____ 5. big   e. few

____ 6. many   f. puts down

Conversation in the Supermarket

Practice the dialog with a partner.

I'm looking for 100% orange juice.

How about this one? It's delicious.

Let me read the Nutrition Facts label.

What does it say?

It has only 10% orange juice.

What is in the other 90%?

It has things we don't want to drink.

Nutrition Facts Label

Read the ingredients on the Nutrition Facts label below. Then answer the questions.

SUN SHINE ORANGE JUICE DRINK
CONTAINS: WATER, HIGH FRUCTOSE CORN SYRUP, ORANGE JUICE, CITRIC ACID, (VITAMIN C), NATURAL FLAVORS, MODIFIED CORNSTARCH, CANOLA OIL, SODIUM CITRATE, SODIUM HEXAMETAPHOSPHATE, SODIUM BENZOATE TO PROTECT FLAVOR, YELLOW #5.
Contains 10% Juice.

---

1. What is the name of the drink? _____

2. What is the first ingredient? _____

3. What is the chemical that protects the flavor? _____

4. What gives the drink its color? _____

5. How much of the drink is orange juice? _____

How much juice is there?

Read each label. Circle the percentage of juice in each product. Write the percentage on the line.

1. ____

2. ____

Problem Solving

My child wants some food from the supermarket that isn't very healthy. What can I do? Put a check next to the good ideas. Write other good ideas on the lines below.

____ buy it one time

____ tell her to buy it with her money

____ read all the ingredients to her

____ look for something healthier

____ tell her it's too expensive

____ show her the chemicals on the label

____ say it isn't very healthy

____ tell her you will buy it another day

____ pretend you don't understand her

____ tell her to eat it at her friend's house

_____   _____

What about you?

Check *Yes* or *No*. Then write the questions and ask your partner.

Yes   No

____ ____ 1. I drink orange juice every morning.

<u>**Do you drink orange juice every morning?**</u>

____ ____ 2. I look at Nutrition Facts labels.

_____

____ ____ 3. I think it's OK to have chemicals in juice.

_____

____ ____ 4. I think it's OK to have dye in juice.

_____

____ ____ 5. I buy only 100% orange juice.

_____

Topics for Discussion or Writing

1. What kind of juice do you buy at the supermarket? What other drinks do you buy?

2. What information do you look at on a Nutrition Facts label?

3. What things don't you want your family to eat or drink? Why?

LESSON 2

Allergic to Shellfish

Mali is at a seafood restaurant. She likes seafood. But there is some seafood that Mali can't eat. She can't eat shellfish. She is **allergic** to it. **Breathing** is difficult when she eats shellfish. She gets a **rash** and an **upset stomach.** It's very dangerous for Mali to eat shrimp, crab, lobster, oysters, clams, and other shellfish. If she eats shellfish, she needs medical help right away.

The waiter comes to take her order. Mali orders grilled halibut. Then she says, "I am allergic to shellfish." Mali also has a message for the cook. "Please tell him to be careful with my dinner." She says that her food can't touch shellfish. She can get very sick from eating a tiny amount. Mali wants the cook to clean the counter, grill, and utensils very well.

"Of course," says the waiter. "I know about **food allergies.** I am allergic to peanuts."

"Okay," says Mali. "I'm glad you understand."

"So you want the grilled halibut," says the waiter. "May I also recommend the crab salad?"

Check *Yes* or *No*.

Yes   No

____ ____ 1. Mali likes seafood.

____ ____ 2. Mali can eat shellfish.

____ ____ 3. Mali is allergic to halibut.

____ ____ 4. Breathing is difficult when she eats shellfish.

____ ____ 5. It's very dangerous for Mali to eat shrimp, crab, and other shellfish.

____ ____ 6. Mali has a message for the cook.

____ ____ 7. Her food can touch shellfish.

____ ____ 8. It's okay for Mali to eat a tiny amount of shellfish.

____ ____ 9. She wants the cook to clean the counter, grill, and utensils very well.

____ ____ 10. The waiter is also allergic to shellfish.

Which category is it?

breathing problems	crab	lobster	swelling
clams	cutting board	rash	upset stomach
counter	grill	shrimp	utensils

Signs of Allergic Reaction   **Things in the Kitchen**   **Shellfish**

1. _____   1. _____   1. _____

2. _____   2. _____   2. _____

3. _____   3. _____   3. _____

4. _____   4. _____   4. _____

Matching: Opposites

____ 1. dangerous   a. easy

____ 2. tiny   b. careless

____ 3. sick   c. unhappy

____ 4. difficult   d. huge

____ 5. careful   e. well

____ 6. glad   f. safe

Conversation in a Restaurant

Practice the dialog with a partner.

Please help me!
What's the matter?
I can't breathe!
I'll call 911 right now.
I think it's an allergic reaction.
What else can I do?
Help me with my medication.

Allergic Reactions to Food

Read the information about allergic reactions to food. Then answer the questions.

Save a Life!

Allergic reactions to food are serious. Call 911 if breathing is difficult. Some people carry epinephrine or emergency medication. Help the person with medication, if necessary. Perform CPR if a person stops breathing. Wait for paramedics to arrive.

1. What is the emergency telephone number? _____

2. When do you call that number? _____

3. What do some people carry? _____

4. What can you help a person with, if necessary? _____

5. When do you perform CPR? _____

Match the words and pictures.

fish	seafood	shellfish

1.

2.

3.

_____   _____   _____

Checklist

Here is part of a menu at a seafood restaurant. Put a check next to the kinds of seafood that Mali can eat. Write other safe seafood items on the lines below.

____ shrimp	____ salmon	____ crab
____ halibut	____ oysters	____ cod
____ scallops	____ tuna	____ lobster
____ swordfish	____ clams	____ mussels
____ lobster	____ trout	____ bass

_____   _____   _____

_____   _____   _____

What about you?

Check *Yes* or *No*. Then write the questions and ask your partner.

Yes   No

____ ____ 1. I like seafood.

Do you like seafood? _____

____ ____ 2. I eat shrimp, crab, lobster, oysters, clams, and other
             shellfish.

             _____

____ ____ 3. I have a food allergy.

             _____

____ ____ 4. I sometimes get a rash and an upset stomach.

             _____

____ ____ 5. I tell people that I am allergic to things.

             _____

Topics for Discussion or Writing

1. What can happen when someone has an allergic reaction to food?

2. How can someone not get sick if he or she has a food allergy?

3. Why is it a good idea to tell people about a food allergy?

LESSON 3

Under Stress

Salman is a restaurant manager. He likes his job, but he works long hours. Salman supports his wife and three children. He worries about money a lot. He worries about paying his bills. He worries about sending his children to college.

Sometimes Salman feels bad. He gets **headaches.** His neck hurts. He grinds his teeth. He doesn't sleep well. On his day off, Salman visits the doctor. He talks about his **symptoms.** Salman has an **exam** and many **tests.** The doctor says, "You are under **stress.** Stress isn't good for you." Then he says, "You are okay, but you need to relax more. Don't work so hard. Have some fun. Take a walk. See a movie."

Salman returns home. "Let's see a movie tonight!" he says. Everyone is happy.

Salman and his family go to the movie theater. "Five tickets, please," says Salman.

"That's $45," says the clerk. Salman rubs his neck. Salman's wife looks at him.

"Don't worry, Salman," she says. "We're having fun. You can grind your teeth on the $6 popcorn."

Check *Yes* or *No.*

Yes   No

____ ____   1. Salman works short hours.

____ ____   2. Salman supports his wife and four children.

____ ____   3. He worries about money a lot.

____ ____   4. Salman gets headaches.

____ ____   5. His back hurts.

____ ____   6. On his day off, Salman visits the doctor.

____ ____   7. The doctor says he is under stress.

____ ____   8. Stress is good for Salman.

____ ____   9. Salman takes his family to college.

____ ____   10. Salman pays $45 for five movie tickets.

Complete each sentence.

gets	says	talks	works
grinds	supports	visits	worries

1. Salman likes his job, but he _____ long hours.

2. He _____ his wife and three children.

3. Salman _____ about money a lot.

4. He _____ headaches.

5. He _____ his teeth.

6. On his day off, Salman _____ the doctor.

7. He _____ about his symptoms.

8. The doctor _____ Salman is under stress.

Matching: Meanings

____ 1. stress   a. signs of a physical problem

____ 2. relax   b. pains in the head

____ 3. headaches   c. to rest and do things that put you at ease

____ 4. college   d. physical or mental pain caused by pressure

____ 5. symptoms   e. a close look by a doctor

____ 6. exam   f. place to study after high school

Conversation with a Doctor

Practice the dialog with a partner.

I'm not feeling well.

What are your symptoms?

I have terrible headaches, and
I grind my teeth.

How are you sleeping?

I don't sleep well at all. I worry a lot.

It sounds like you're under stress.

Is there anything I can do?

Do things that help you relax.

Problems with Stress

Read the information the doctor gave Salman about stress. Then answer the questions.

Are you worrying about your job, money, family,
illness, retirement, or the death of a family member?
Are you working a lot? Perhaps you are under stress.
Stress can affect your health. It can cause minor
problems like insomnia, backaches, or headaches.
It can also cause serious problems like high blood
pressure and heart disease.

1. What things can cause stress?

2. What can stress affect?

3. What minor problems can stress cause?

4. What serious problems can stress cause?

Sequence the pictures.

Listen and number the pictures in the correct order.

a. _____

c. _____

b. _____

d. _____

Problem Solving

I am under stress. I need to relax more. What can I do? Put a check next to the good ideas. Write other good ideas on the lines below.

_____ see a movie   _____ worry about money

_____ take a walk   _____ visit friends

_____ drink alcohol   _____ take a day off work

_____ meditate   _____ have arguments

_____ eat a healthy diet   _____ exercise

_____   _____

_____   _____

What about you?

Check *Yes* or *No*. Then write the questions and ask your partner.

Yes   No

_____ _____ 1. I worry about money a lot.

Do you worry about money a lot? _____

_____ _____ 2. I get headaches.

_____

_____ _____ 3. I grind my teeth.

_____

_____ _____ 4. I sleep well.

_____

_____ _____ 5. I see a movie when I need to relax.

_____

Topics for Discussion or Writing

1. What things do you worry about?

2. Are you ever under stress? If so, what symptoms do you have?
   How do you relax?

3. How can a family see a movie without paying a lot of money?

LESSON 4

A Heavy Box

Adam has a new job in a large warehouse. Adam has to lift many boxes in his job. Some of the boxes are light. Some of the boxes are heavy. Right now there is a heavy box on the floor. Adam needs to move it. He bends over to pick it up. His legs are straight. Nick, his supervisor, sees him. "No, Adam!" says Nick. "You can **hurt** your **back!**"

Nick picks up a light box. He shows Adam how to lift it. "First, squat down," he says. "Bend at your **hips** and **knees** only. Lift slowly. Hold the box close to your body. Take small steps. Squat down again when you put the box down. Bend only at your hips and knees."

"Thanks," says Adam. "I appreciate you telling me that."

"You're welcome," says Nick. "Always ask for help when something is too heavy."

"Okay," says Adam. "This box is too heavy. Can you give me a hand?"

"Sorry," says Nick. "I don't want to hurt my back."

Check **Yes** or **No**.

Yes No

____ ____ 1. Adam has a new job in a large warehouse.

____ ____ 2. All of the boxes in the warehouse are heavy.

____ ____ 3. Right now Adam needs to lift a heavy box.

____ ____ 4. His legs are straight.

____ ____ 5. Nick, Adam's supervisor, sees him.

____ ____ 6. Nick says, "You can hurt your hips!"

____ ____ 7. Nick picks up a heavy box.

____ ____ 8. Nick says, "Bend at your hips and knees only."

____ ____ 9. Nick says to lift quickly and take big steps.

____ ____ 10. Nick helps Adam move the heavy box.

Complete each sentence.

body	floor	knees	steps
boxes	help	legs	supervisor

1. Adam has to lift many _____ in his job.

2. Right now there is a heavy box on the _____.

3. Adam bends over to pick it up. His _____ are straight.

4. Nick, his _____, says, "No, Adam!"

5. Nick says to bend at the hips and _____ only.

6. He tells Adam to hold the box close to his _____.

7. Adam needs to take small _____.

8. Adam asks for _____, but Nick doesn't want to hurt his back.

Matching: Opposites

____ 1. large   a. few

____ 2. heavy   b. stand up

____ 3. slowly   c. small

____ 4. many   d. far away

____ 5. bend over   e. light

____ 6. close   f. quickly

Conversation in the Warehouse

Practice the dialog with a partner.

Can you please move that box?

Which box?

It's that one over there on the floor.

Ugh. It's too heavy. I can't lift it.

Do you need a hand?

Sure. I don't want to hurt my back.

Let's lift it together.

Thanks. I appreciate your help.

Lifting a Heavy Box

Read the information on lifting a heavy box safely. Then circle the picture of each worker who is lifting safely.

> - Squat down. Bend at your hips and knees only.
> - Lift the box slowly.
> - Hold the box close to your body.
> - Take small steps.
> - Put down the box. Squat with hips and knees again.

1.

2.

3.

Listen. Check the correct picture.

1.

a. _____   b. _____

3.

a. _____   b. _____

2.

a. _____   b. _____

Problem Solving

I need to move a very heavy box. What can I do? Put a check next to the good ideas. Write other good ideas on the lines below.

_____ ask for help   _____ open the box and take some things out

_____ get a dolly   _____ kick it with my foot

_____ lift it without help   _____ lift it with my legs straight

_____ wear a back brace   _____ pull it with a rope

_____ get a forklift   _____ wait for someone to help me

_____   _____

_____   _____

What about you?

Check *Yes* or *No*. Then write the questions and ask your partner.

Yes   No

____ ____   1. I lift boxes at work.

          Do you lift boxes at work? _____

____ ____   2. I sometimes lift other heavy things.

          _____

____ ____   3. I bend at my hips and knees only.

          _____

____ ____   4. I hold heavy things close to my body and take small steps.

          _____

____ ____   5. I ask for help when I need it.

          _____

Topics for Discussion or Writing

1. In what ways can you hurt your back?

2. What heavy things do you sometimes need to lift or move?

3. Who can you ask for help at work or at home?

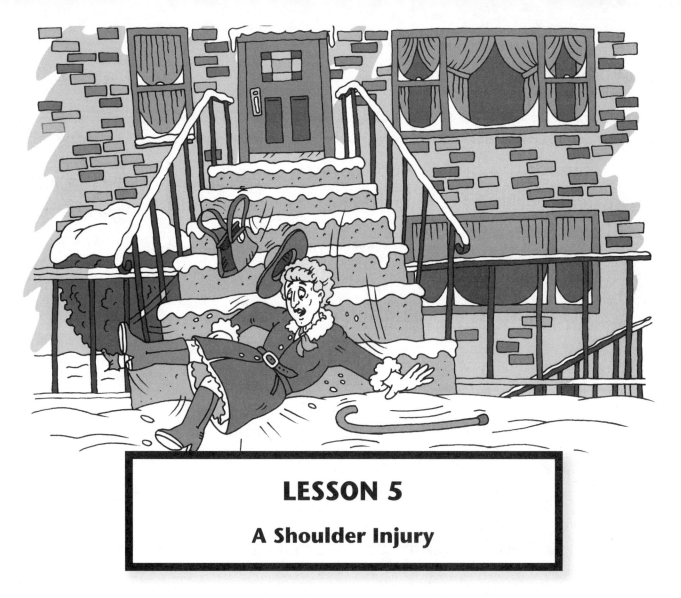

LESSON 5

A Shoulder Injury

Julia is 73 years old. Julia is walking down her front steps. It is winter, and the steps are icy. Julia slips on some ice. She falls and hurts her shoulder. The **shoulder** is very **painful.** Julia has shoulder **surgery.** After the surgery, her doctor gives her directions. Julia needs to rest her shoulder. She can't sweep or vacuum. For six weeks, she can't lift anything heavier than a coffee cup.

Her doctor also wants her to go to **physical therapy.** Julia goes three times a week. Her physical therapist helps Julia with special exercises for her shoulder. Julia stretches. She uses weights and pulleys. Her shoulder gets stronger. Julia feels better too. She likes exercise. She also likes to have her husband sweep and vacuum.

After four months, Julia's doctor says she is OK. She can stop going to physical therapy. "Continue your exercises at home," says the doctor. "You can sweep and vacuum. But be careful on the steps. You don't want another surgery."

"I don't want to sweep and vacuum," says Julia. "My husband can do that. When can I start swimming?"

Check *Yes* or *No*.

Yes   No

____ ____   1. Julia is 75 years old.

____ ____   2. She falls and hurts her shoulder.

____ ____   3. Julia has shoulder surgery.

____ ____   4. Julia can lift three coffee cups.

____ ____   5. Julia goes to physical therapy three times a week.

____ ____   6. She stretches and uses weights and pulleys.

____ ____   7. Julia likes exercise.

____ ____   8. After six months, Julia's doctor says she is OK.

____ ____   9. Julia wants to sweep and vacuum.

____ ____   10. Julia's husband wants to start swimming.

Which category is it?

bathtub	floor	physical therapist	surgeon
doctor	husband	rest	therapy
exercise	patio	steps	weights

Things that Help Julia

1. _____

2. _____

3. _____

4. _____

People who Help Julia

1. _____

2. _____

3. _____

4. _____

Places to Slip

1. _____

2. _____

3. _____

4. _____

Matching: Meanings

____ 1. swimming   a. frozen water

____ 2. directions   b. operation on the body

____ 3. shoulder   c. moving in water

____ 4. painful   d. body part between the neck and upper arm

____ 5. ice   e. instructions

____ 6. surgery   f. hurting

Conversation with a Doctor after Surgery

Practice the dialog with a partner.

I have some directions for you.

What are they?

You need to rest your shoulder. No housework.

Can I lift anything?

Don't lift anything heavier than a coffee cup.

Anything else?

You need physical therapy three times a week.

Getting Physical Therapy

Read the physical therapy information. Then answer the questions.

LAKESHORE PHYSICAL THERAPY GROUP

Adults • Pediatrics • Women's Health

Post-surgery care • Joint and Muscle Pain • Sports and Work Injuries

One-on-One Treatment • Exercise and Conditioning • Massage Therapy

Most Insurance Accepted

5671 LAKESHORE DRIVE • (714) 555-9348 • MONDAY-FRIDAY 7:00 AM TO 6:00 PM

---

1. What problems can the physical therapists help? _____

_____

2. What is the address? _____

3. What is the telephone number? _____

4. What are the hours? _____

Sequence the pictures.

Listen and number the pictures in the correct order.

a. ____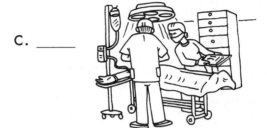

c. ____

b. ____

d. ____

Checklist

Julia is home after her shoulder surgery. Put a check next to the things that are good for her to use. Write other things she can use on the lines below.

____ pain medication

____ physical therapist information

____ a vacuum

____ a coffee cup

____ a swimming pool

____ a bell to ring for her husband

____ a comfortable chair

____ doctor's telephone number

____ weights

____ rest

_____

_____

_____

_____

What about you?

Check *Yes* or *No*. Then write the questions and ask your partner.

Yes   No

____ ____   1. I have a shoulder injury.

Do you have a shoulder injury? _____

____ ____   2. I follow directions a doctor gives me.

_____

____ ____   3. I like to sweep and vacuum.

_____

____ ____   4. I like swimming.

_____

____ ____   5. I exercise three times a week.

_____

Topics for Discussion or Writing

1. How can you go down steps so you don't slip?

2. Do you have an injury? If so, how do you take care of it?

3. What kind of exercise do you usually do? How does exercise make you feel?

LESSON 6

Flossing Helps

Eric takes very good care of his **teeth.** He has a healthy **diet.** He avoids sugary sodas and sweets. He brushes his teeth twice a day. He uses **fluoride** toothpaste. Eric also visits his **dentist** regularly. Everyone thinks Eric has a beautiful smile.

Right now Eric is having a dental exam. "You have a lot of **plaque,"** says the dentist. "That's a film on your teeth where **bacteria** can grow. Do you **floss?"**

"No," answers Eric. "Do I need to floss?"

"Yes," says the dentist. She explains that plaque can cause tooth **decay** and **gum** disease. "A toothbrush can't clean all areas," she says. "Flossing helps remove plaque between the teeth." Then the dentist takes about 18 inches of **dental floss.** She gently cleans between Eric's teeth.

"Thank you," says Eric. "My teeth feel a lot better."

"You're welcome," says the dentist. "Take the dental floss with you. Use it every day. You want to keep your beautiful smile."

Eric smiles at the dentist. "See you in six months," he says. "I promise to floss regularly."

Check *Yes* or *No*.

Yes   No

____ ____   1. Eric takes very good care of his teeth.

____ ____   2. He has a lot of sugary sodas and sweets.

____ ____   3. He brushes his teeth once a day.

____ ____   4. Eric flosses before his dental exam.

____ ____   5. He has a lot of plaque.

____ ____   6. Plaque can cause tooth decay and gum disease.

____ ____   7. A toothbrush can clean all areas.

____ ____   8. The dentist takes about eight inches of dental floss.

____ ____   9. She gently cleans between Eric's teeth.

____ ____   10. Eric wants to keep his beautiful smile.

Which category is it?

candy	dental exam	plaque	sweetened juice
cavities	dental floss	soda	toothbrush
decay	gum disease	sugar	toothpaste

Things that Help Teeth

1. _____

2. _____

3. _____

4. _____

Dental Problems

1. _____

2. _____

3. _____

4. _____

Food and Drinks to Avoid

1. _____

2. _____

3. _____

4. _____

Matching: Meanings

_____ 1. dentist   a. to take away

_____ 2. diet   b. a doctor for teeth

_____ 3. remove   c. without causing pain

_____ 4. smile   d. a film on teeth where bacteria can grow

_____ 5. plaque   e. the food you eat

_____ 6. gently   f. a happy expression showing teeth

Conversation with the Dentist

Practice the dialog with a partner.

You have a lot of plaque.

I do?

Yes. Do you floss?

No. But I brush my teeth twice a day.

A toothbrush can't clean all areas.

What does flossing do?

Flossing helps remove plaque between
the teeth.

Okay. I'll floss.

Using Dental Floss

Read how Eric uses dental floss at home. Then answer the questions.

> ◆ Eric takes 18 inches of dental floss and winds it around
>   his middle fingers.
> ◆ He gently cleans between his teeth and along the gumline.
> ◆ He moves the floss to a clean section each time.
> ◆ Eric flosses one or more times a day.

1. How much dental floss does Eric use? _____

2. Where does he wind it? _____

3. Where does he clean? _____

4. Where does he move the floss each time? _____

5. How often does he floss? _____

Match the words and pictures.

dental exam	dental floss	fluoride toothpaste

1.

2.

3.

_____   _____   _____

Problem Solving

I don't want tooth decay and gum disease. What can I do? Put a check next to the good ideas. Write other good ideas on the lines below.

____ brush my teeth twice a day   ____ use dental floss every day

____ visit the dentist regularly   ____ eat sweets

____ smoke   ____ have a healthy diet

____ drink sugary sodas   ____ drink coffee

____ use mouthwash   ____ use fluoride toothpaste

_____   _____

What about you?

Check *Yes* or *No*. Then write the questions and ask your partner.

Yes   No

____ ____ 1. I take good care of my teeth.

   <u>*Do you take good care of your teeth?*</u>

____ ____ 2. I have a healthy diet.

   _____

____ ____ 3. I avoid sugary sodas and sweets.

   _____

____ ____ 4. I brush my teeth twice a day.

   _____

____ ____ 5. I floss one or more times a day.

   _____

Topics for Discussion or Writing

1. How often do you visit the dentist? Why is it important to go regularly?

2. What happens at a dental exam?

3. What kind of toothpaste do you use? What does it do?

LESSON 7

Two Cutting Boards

Svetlana and her daughter, Alina, are making soup. Alina wants to cut up the chicken and vegetables. First Alina washes her **hands** with warm, soapy water. Then she puts the chicken on a plastic cutting board. She cuts the chicken into small pieces. Svetlana reminds Alina to wash her hands again. Then Alina picks up the vegetables. She almost puts them down on the same cutting board. "No!" says Svetlana. "Don't use the same cutting board for meat and vegetables!"

"Why not?" asks Alina.

"The chicken can have **bacteria,**" answers Svetlana. "We don't want to get sick. We need to keep **raw** meat away from other food." Svetlana hands Alina a different cutting board.

Then Svetlana washes the plastic cutting board, knife, and counter with hot, soapy water. Next she puts one teaspoon of **chlorine bleach** in one quart of water. She rinses everything with it. Svetlana dries her hands on a kitchen towel. She puts the towel next to the stove.

"Put the towel in the laundry, Mom." says Alina. "We don't want to get sick."

Check *Yes* or *No*.

Yes   No

_____ _____ 1. Svetlana and Alina are making soap.

_____ _____ 2. Alina wants to cut up the chicken and vegetables.

_____ _____ 3. First Alina washes her hands with one teaspoon of chlorine bleach.

_____ _____ 4. Alina puts the chicken on a plastic cutting board.

_____ _____ 5. Alina almost puts the vegetables on the same cutting board.

_____ _____ 6. Svetlana says to use the same cutting board.

_____ _____ 7. Chicken can have bacteria.

_____ _____ 8. Svetlana washes the plastic cutting board, knife, and counter.

_____ _____ 9. She rinses everything with one quart of chlorine bleach.

_____ _____ 10. Svetlana dries her hands on a kitchen towel.

Complete each sentence.

chlorine	hot	plastic	small
different	kitchen	raw	soapy

1. Alina washes her hands with warm, _____ water.

2. Then she puts the chicken on a _____ cutting board.

3. Alina cuts the chicken into _____ pieces.

4. Svetlana tells Alina to keep _____ meat away from other food.

5. She hands Alina a _____ cutting board.

6. She washes everything with _____, soapy water.

7. She rinses everything with one teaspoon of _____ bleach in one quart of water.

8. She dries her hands on a _____ towel.

Matching: Meanings

____ 1. teaspoon

____ 2. raw

____ 3. bacteria

____ 4. chlorine bleach

____ 5. quart

a. a chemical for cleaning

b. germs

c. small spoon used for measuring

d. 32 ounces or 4 cups

e. not cooked

Conversation in the Kitchen

Practice the dialog with a partner.

Don't use the same cutting board for raw meat and vegetables!

Why not?

That raw chicken can have bacteria.

What can I use?

Use a different cutting board.

Is this one OK?

Sure. Just keep raw meat away from other food.

Right. We don't want to get sick.

Cleaning a Cutting Board

Read about cleaning a cutting board. Then answer the questions.

- Wash the cutting board with hot, soapy water.
- Put the cutting board through the automatic dishwasher or rinse it in a solution of one teaspoon of chlorine bleach in one quart of water.
- Always wash and sanitize a cutting board after using it for raw foods.
- Have one cutting board for raw meat or fish and another for other foods.

1. What do you use to wash the cutting board? _____

2. How much bleach and water do you use to rinse it? _____

3. When do you wash and sanitize a cutting board? _____

4. How many cutting boards is it good to have? _____

Label the items.

chicken	cutting board	towel
counter	knife	vegetables

1. _____

2. _____

3. _____

4. _____

5. _____

6. _____

Checklist

You don't want to get sick. Put a check next to the things that kill germs in the kitchen. Write other things you can use on the lines below.

____ chlorine bleach

____ soap and water

____ disinfecting wipes

____ antibacterial cleaners

____ raw chicken

____ a dirty sponge

____ paper towels

____ bacteria

____ hot water

____ liquid detergent

_____   _____

_____   _____

What about you?

Check *Yes* or *No*. Then write the questions and ask your partner.

Yes   No

____ ____   1. I wash my hands with warm, soapy water.

   Do you wash your hands with warm, soapy water?

____ ____   2. I use different cutting boards for meat and vegetables.

_____

____ ____   3. I wash my cutting board with hot, soapy water.

_____

____ ____   4. I put my cutting board through the dishwasher.

_____

____ ____   5. I rinse my cutting board with one teaspoon of bleach in one quart of water.

_____

Topics for Discussion or Writing

1. How do you clean different areas in your kitchen? Which products do you use?

2. What foods can have dangerous bacteria?

3. What can you do if you get sick from eating bad food?

LESSON 8

Getting a Refill

Ted has **asthma.** Sometimes it's hard for Ted to **breathe.** He takes asthma **medication** every day.

On Monday, Ted opens his medicine cabinet. He has very little medication. He needs to call the **pharmacy** for a **refill.** "I can do that later," says Ted. But Ted forgets. He also forgets to call on Tuesday and Wednesday. On Thursday, Ted opens his medicine cabinet again. He has no more asthma medication.

Ted calls the pharmacy. "I need a refill for my asthma medication."

The assistant asks for Ted's name and **prescription** number. Then she says, "I'm sorry. You have no more refills. We need to call or fax your doctor's office for a new prescription. You can probably pick up your medication on Saturday."

"No," says Ted. "I don't have any more medication. I need to take it every day. I can't wait."

"Please tell your doctor to call us right away," says the assistant.

Ted hangs up the phone. It's 3:00 now. The doctor's office closes at 5:00. Ted says, "I can do that later."

Check *Yes* or *No*.

Yes   No

____ ____ 1. Ted has asthma.

____ ____ 2. He takes medication every day.

____ ____ 3. Ted has a lot of medication on Monday.

____ ____ 4. Ted forgets to call the pharmacy on Wednesday.

____ ____ 5. On Thursday, Ted has no more medication.

____ ____ 6. The assistant at the pharmacy asks for Ted's address.

____ ____ 7. Ted has one more refill.

____ ____ 8. Ted can wait until Saturday for a new prescription.

____ ____ 9. The assistant tells Ted that his doctor has to call right away.

____ ____ 10. Ted hangs up the phone and calls his doctor.

Which category is it?

allergies	doctor's name	medication	prescription number
aspirin	eye drops	patient's name	smoking
asthma	lung diseases	pharmacy phone number	thermometer

Information on Medicine Packages	Causes of Breathing Problems	Things in a Medicine Cabinet
1. _____	1. _____	1. _____
2. _____	2. _____	2. _____
3. _____	3. _____	3. _____
4. _____	4. _____	4. _____

Matching: Meanings

____ 1. pharmacy   a. more of the same medication

____ 2. breathe   b. to not remember

____ 3. medication   c. to take air into and out of the lungs

____ 4. refill   d. a store or part of a store that sells medications

____ 5. prescription   e. a doctor's order for medication

____ 6. forget   f. medicine

Conversation with the Doctor's Office

Practice the dialog with a partner.

I need more asthma medication.

Can you call my pharmacy?

What's your name?

My name is Ted Chu.

Which pharmacy?

It's the Save-More pharmacy on L Street.

Do you have their number?

Yes, it's 555-1489.

Okay, we'll call it in. But you need to see the doctor this month.

A Medication Label

Read the label for Ted's medication. Then answer the questions.

```
SAVE-MORE PHARMACY
2650 L Street
24 Hour Phone (212) 555-1489

Rx 1091164              Taylor, Gloria MD

CHU, TED
Use as Directed

BREATHE-EASY           0 REFILLS
```

1. What is the prescription number? _____

2. What is the doctor's name? _____

3. What is the address of the pharmacy? _____

4. What is the patient's name? _____

5. How many refills does he have left? _____

Sequence the pictures.

Listen and number the pictures in the correct order.

a. ____

c. ____

b. ____

d. ____

Problem Solving

I need some medication. The pharmacy says I don't have any refills. What can I do? Put a check next to the good ideas. Write other good ideas on the lines below.

____ call my doctor right away

____ call 911

____ take my friend's medication

____ go to my doctor's office

____ ask the pharmacist for help

____ stop taking my medication

____ go to a 24-hour clinic for a new prescription

____ ask the pharmacy to fax my doctor

____ buy some over-the-counter medicine

____ get angry with the pharmacy assistant

What about you?

Check *Yes* or *No*. Then write the questions and ask your partner.

Yes   No

___ ___ 1. I take medication every day.

Do you take medication every day?
_____

___ ___ 2. I have medication in my medicine cabinet.

_____

___ ___ 3. I sometimes call a pharmacy about a prescription.

_____

___ ___ 4. I sometimes call my doctor about a prescription.

_____

___ ___ 5. I read medication labels to see if I have refills.

_____

Topics for Discussion or Writing

1. For what things can you take medication every day?

2. What do you need to know when you call the pharmacy for a refill?

3. When do you call the pharmacy for a refill? Why is it not good to wait until you have no more medication?

LESSON 9

Calling Poison Control

Kate's son Connor is four years old. Every morning Kate gives Connor a children's **vitamin.** Connor likes the vitamins. They look like cartoon characters. They taste good. Connor says, "Yum. Can I have another one?"

"Tomorrow," says Kate. "Only one a day." She puts on the **child-resistant** cap. Then she puts the vitamins on the top shelf of the kitchen cabinet. It's dangerous for children to eat too many vitamins.

This morning Kate gives Connor a vitamin. Then the telephone rings. Kate forgets to put on the child-resistant cap. She puts the vitamins on the counter and answers the telephone. Kate isn't watching Connor. Connor picks up the open bottle and runs. After a few minutes, Kate hangs up the telephone. She looks for Connor. He is in his room chewing vitamins.

"Oh no!" says Kate. She is very upset. The vitamin bottle is almost empty. She thinks Connor ate about 20 vitamins. Kate runs to the telephone to call the **Poison** Control Center.

"Yum," says Connor. "Can I have another one tomorrow?"

Check *Yes* or *No*.

Yes   No

___ ___ 1. Every morning Kate gives Connor a children's vitamin.

___ ___ 2. The vitamins look like cartoon characters.

___ ___ 3. They taste terrible.

___ ___ 4. It's dangerous for children to eat too many vitamins.

___ ___ 5. This morning Kate forgets to put on the child-resistant cap.

___ ___ 6. She puts the vitamins on the top shelf and answers the telephone.

___ ___ 7. Kate is watching Connor while she talks on the telephone.

___ ___ 8. Connor is in his room chewing vitamins.

___ ___ 9. She thinks Connor ate about two vitamins.

___ ___ 10. Kate runs to the telephone to call the Poison Control Center.

Complete each sentence.

| forgets | hangs up | puts | runs |
| gives | picks up | rings | thinks |

1. This morning Kate _____ Connor a vitamin.

2. Then the telephone _____.

3. Kate _____ to put on the child-resistant cap.

4. She _____ the vitamins on the counter.

5. Connor _____ the open bottle and runs.

6. After a few minutes, Kate _____ the telephone.

7. Kate is upset. She _____ Connor ate about 20 vitamins.

8. Kate _____ to the telephone to call the Poison Control Center.

Matching: Meanings

_____ 1. child-resistant   a. container

_____ 2. bottle   b. the highest

_____ 3. top   c. a pill with substances for good health

_____ 4. poison   d. having nothing inside

_____ 5. empty   e. difficult for a child to open

_____ 6. vitamin   f. something that can kill you

Conversation with a Poison Control Operator

Practice the dialog with a partner.

My son just ate a lot of vitamins!

Does he have any symptoms?

No, but he only ate them about five minutes ago.

How old is he?

He's four years old.

How much does he weigh?

He weighs 42 pounds.

What kind of vitamins?

They were the Dancing Dog Vitamins.

Directions for Taking Vitamins

Read the directions on the bottle of vitamins. Then answer the questions.

> # DANCING DOG
> ## Complete Multivitamins
>
> **Directions:** Children 4 years of age and older: Chew one tablet daily. Keep this product out of the reach of children. In case of accidental overdose, call a doctor or poison control center immediately. Child-Resistant Cap: Do not take vitamins if the safety seal is torn or missing.

1. How many tablets a day can a child have? _____

2. Where do you keep this product? _____

3. Who can you call in case of accidental overdose? _____

4. When should you not take these vitamins? _____

Sequence the pictures.

Listen and number the pictures in the correct order.

a. ____

b. ____

c. ____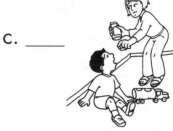

d. ____

Checklist

People call Poison Control Centers about items like the ones below. Put a check next to the ones that you have in your home. Write other possibly dangerous items on the lines below.

____ bleach   ____ mouthwash   ____ medications

____ furniture polish   ____ medication   ____ dishwasher detergent

____ vitamins   ____ cigarettes   ____ ammonia

____ alcohol   ____ plants   ____ cough syrup

____ silica gel   ____ mercury   ____ insecticide

_____   _____   _____

_____   _____   _____

What about you?

Check *Yes* or *No*. Then write the questions and ask your partner.

Yes   No

____ ____   1. I take vitamins every day.

   Do you take vitamins every day? _____

____ ____   2. I give vitamins to my child.

   _____

____ ____   3. I always put on child-resistant caps.

   _____

____ ____   4. I watch my child when I am on the telephone.

   _____

____ ____   5. I have a telephone number for the Poison Control Center.

   _____

Topics for Discussion or Writing

1. Do you have dangerous products in your home? If so, where do you put them?

2. For what reasons should you call a Poison Control Center?

3. Why do children sometimes want things that are dangerous?

LESSON 10

Packing for the Hospital

Greta is packing a suitcase for her father. He is going to the **hospital** today. He needs to be there for a few days. Greta packs his pajamas, slippers, and bathrobe. She adds a razor, soap, shampoo, a toothbrush, toothpaste, and other personal items. Then she puts his **health insurance** information in her purse.

Greta remembers two other very important things. The first is her father's **medications.** Greta gets all his **prescription drugs** in their original containers. The second is a list of her father's **allergies.** He is **allergic** to two **antibiotics.** He is also allergic to strawberries. The hospital staff needs to know that.

Later Greta's father is admitted to the hospital. Greta sits next to her father in his room. She shows the medications and the allergy list to the doctors and nurses. They record everything on his **chart.** They appreciate Greta's help.

Greta pats her father's hand. "You're all set, Dad," she says.

"Very good," says Greta's father. "Can you go down to the gift shop? I want something to read."

Check *Yes* or *No*.

Yes   No

_____ _____ 1. Greta is packing a suitcase for her mother.

_____ _____ 2. Her father is going to the hospital today.

_____ _____ 3. Greta packs his pajamas, slippers, and bathrobe.

_____ _____ 4. Greta puts his health insurance information in her purse.

_____ _____ 5. She puts his prescription drugs in small plastic bags.

_____ _____ 6. Greta's father is allergic to three antibiotics.

_____ _____ 7. He is also allergic to blueberries.

_____ _____ 8. Greta shows everything to the doctors and nurses.

_____ _____ 9. They record everything on his chart.

_____ _____ 10. Greta packs something for her father to read.

Which category is it?

bathrobe	nightgown	razor	social worker
dietician	nurse	shampoo	toothbrush
doctor	pajamas	slippers	toothpaste

Hospital Staff

1. _____
2. _____
3. _____
4. _____

Personal Items

1. _____
2. _____
3. _____
4. _____

Clothing for the Hospital

1. _____
2. _____
3. _____
4. _____

Matching: Meanings

____ 1. suitcase

____ 2. gift shop

____ 3. razor

____ 4. antibiotics

____ 5. chart

____ 6. insurance

a. place in a hospital to buy things

b. item used for shaving

c. place to record medical information

d. case for carrying clothes and personal items

e. company or plan that helps pay hospital bills

f. drugs used to cure infections

Conversation with a Hospital Nurse

Practice the dialog with a partner.

Is your father taking any medication?

Yes, he is. I have it right here.

Thanks. Any allergies?

Yes, he is allergic to two antibiotics.

Do you know what they are?

Yes. They are on this list.

How about food allergies?

He can't eat strawberries.

An Insurance Card

Look at the health insurance card for Greta's father. Then answer the questions. Write your answers on the lines.

> ✚ **Green Cross HMO** ✚
>
> **Group** 555100H999
> **Member ID** ABC 098H76543
> **Rolf Schmidt**   MED PLAN: H3
>
> MED OFFICE: Coast Medical Group
> **Physician:** Dong Hieu
>   (619) 555-6720

1. What is Greta's father's name? _____

2. What is the name of the insurance company? _____

3. Who is his physician? _____

4. What is his physician's telephone number? _____

Label the items.

1. _____

2. _____

3. _____

4. _____

5. _____

6. _____

7. _____

8. _____

9. _____

Checklist

You want to give information about someone to hospital staff. Put a check next to the things the staff needs to know about the person. Write other important information on the lines below.

_____ medical history

_____ insurance information

_____ likes to read

_____ food allergies

_____ needs a translator

_____ allergies to medication

_____ religion

_____ emergency contact

_____ current x-rays

_____ special diet

_____

_____

_____

_____

What about you?

Check *Yes* or *No*. Then write the questions and ask your partner.

Yes   No

____ ____ 1. I help someone when they go to the hospital.

Do you help someone when they go to the hospital?

____ ____ 2. I have health insurance.

_____

____ ____ 3. I have prescription drugs.

_____

____ ____ 4. I have allergies to some antibiotics.

_____

____ ____ 5. I have allergies to some foods.

_____

Topics for Discussion or Writing

1. What are some things that are not good to pack for the hospital? Why?

2. What are the names of the hospitals in your area? Do you need health insurance to go there?

3. What are some things you can buy in a hospital gift shop?

LESSON 11

Talking about Alcohol

Shen doesn't want his son to drink **alcohol.** His son, Chang, is 17 years old. He is a teenager. Shen talks about alcohol a lot. He tells Chang that drinking is dangerous. "Teenagers don't make good decisions when they drink alcohol," says Shen. "It isn't safe and it isn't legal."

Shen also talks about drinking and driving. It's very bad. Alcohol affects a person's **vision** and **hearing. Reactions** are slower. Drinking alcohol causes accidents. Chang promises never to drink and drive. But sometimes Chang is a passenger in another teenager's car. Does that teenager drink alcohol? Shen doesn't know all of Chang's friends. He doesn't know their parents. Shen feels very nervous when Chang is riding with other teenagers.

Shen always gives Chang money for transportation. He reminds Chang to call him any time. "Never ride with someone who is drinking," says Shen. "I can always pick you up. No questions. I promise."

"Okay, Dad," says Chang. "You can trust me."

"Good," says Shen. "I trust you. But I don't trust alcohol."

Check *Yes* or *No*.

Yes   No

____	____	1. Shen wants his son to drink alcohol.
____	____	2. Chang is a teenager.
____	____	3. Shen tells Chang that drinking is dangerous.
____	____	4. Teenage drinking is safe and legal.
____	____	5. Alcohol affects a person's vision and hearing.
____	____	6. Alcohol causes accidents.
____	____	7. Chang wants to drink and drive.
____	____	8. Shen knows all of Chang's friends and their parents.
____	____	9. Shen always gives Chang money for transportation.
____	____	10. Shen trusts alcohol.

Complete each sentence.

accidents	friends	passenger	teenager
alcohol	money	questions	vision

1. Chang is 17 years old. He is a _____.

2. Shen, his father, doesn't want him to drink _____.

3. Alcohol affects a person's _____ and hearing.

4. It causes _____.

5. Sometimes Chang is a _____ in another teenager's car.

6. Shen doesn't know all of Chang's _____.

7. Shen always gives Chang _____ for transportation.

8. Shen says, "I can always pick you up. No _____."

Matching: Opposites

____	1. nervous	a. daughter
____	2. son	b. calm
____	3. always	c. drop off
____	4. trust	d. feel suspicious
____	5. legal	e. never
____	6. pick up	f. unlawful

Conversation with a School Counselor

Practice the dialog with a partner.

I worry about my son drinking and driving.

Do you talk about it at home?

Yes. But my son rides with friends a lot.

Get to know his friends and their parents.

Is there anything else I can do?

Always give him money for transportation.

Do you have any other ideas?

Tell him he can call you any time.

Teenagers and Alcohol

Read the information about teenagers and alcohol. Then answer the questions.

> Teenagers have more car accidents after drinking alcohol than adults. There are many teenage drinkers. Alcohol is the most common drug used by teenagers. Nearly 50% of 17-year-olds drink at least once a month. Nearly 7.2 million teenagers also binge drink. That means they have five or more drinks at the same time.

1. What group has more accidents after drinking alcohol? _____

2. What is the most common drug used by teenagers? _____

3. What percentage of teenagers drink once a month? _____

4. What do 7.2 million teenagers do? _____

Listen. Check the correct picture.

1.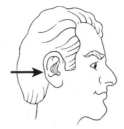

a. ____ b. ____

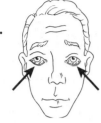 

a. ____ b. ____

2.

a. ____ b. ____

Problem Solving

I don't want my teenager to ride with someone who is drinking. Put a check next to the good ideas. Write other good ideas on the lines below.

____ give him money for transportation

____ always pick him up

____ talk about alcohol a lot

____ trust him

____ follow him in my car

____ trust all of his friends

____ let him drink at home

____ meet his friends and their parents

____ ask a lot of questions

____ give him a cell phone

_____

_____

_____

_____

What about you?

Check *Yes* or *No*. Then write the questions and ask your partner.

Yes   No

____ ____   1. I have a teenaged child.

<u>Do you have a teenaged child?</u>

____ ____   2. I talk about alcohol a lot.

_____

____ ____   3. I think that drinking is dangerous.

_____

____ ____   4. I think drinking and driving is very bad.

_____

____ ____   5. I sometimes ride with people who are drinking and driving.

_____

Topics for Discussion or Writing

1. What important things should parents talk about with their children?

2. Do you have children? If so, do you feel nervous if your child is a passenger in a teenager's car? Why or why not?

3. What do you do if you think someone is drinking and driving?

LESSON 12

A Child with Pink Eye

Rachel is four years old. She is sitting in her preschool office. Her mother is picking her up early. Rachel's mom needs to take her home. Rachel's left eye is very red and **itchy.** She is rubbing it a lot. "It looks like **conjunctivitis,** or pink eye," says the preschool director. "Several other children have the same **infection.** It spreads easily."

At home, Rachel's mother makes an **appointment** to see the **pediatrician.** He can see her at 1:00 P.M. Doctor Linzer examines Rachel's eye. It has some thick yellow **discharge.** He says her infection is **bacterial.** He writes Rachel's mother a prescription for some **antibiotic eye drops.** Rachel needs to get the drops for one week.

"This infection is very **contagious,**" says Doctor Linzer. "Keep your hands clean. Wash them a lot. Use warm water and soap." Rachel rubs her eye again. "And don't touch your eyes with your hands, Rachel," says the doctor. "Do you understand?"

Rachel reaches up and touches her mother's eyes. "I understand," says Rachel. "Don't do that."

Check *Yes* or *No.*

Yes   No

____ ____ 1. Rachel is four years old.

____ ____ 2. Her mother is picking her up early.

____ ____ 3. Rachel's right eye is very red and itchy.

____ ____ 4. It looks like conjunctivitis, or pink eye.

____ ____ 5. Only one other child has the same infection.

____ ____ 6. Doctor Linzer examines Rachel's ear.

____ ____ 7. He writes a prescription for some antibiotic eye drops.

____ ____ 8. Rachel needs to get the drops for one month.

____ ____ 9. This infection is very contagious.

____ ____ 10. Rachel needs to wash her hands a lot.

Complete each sentence.

conjunctivitis	eye	hands	pediatrician
discharge	eye drops	infection	preschool

1. Rachel's left _____ is very red and itchy.

2. Her mother needs to take her home from _____.

3. It looks like _____, or pink eye.

4. The _____ can see her at 1:00.

5. Rachel's eye has some thick yellow _____.

6. Doctor Linzer says her _____ is bacterial.

7. Rachel needs to get antibiotic _____ for one week.

8. Rachel can't touch her eyes with her _____.

Matching: Meanings

____ 1. contagious   a. school before kindergarten

____ 2. discharge   b. to feel with the hand

____ 3. preschool   c. fluid that comes out of a body part

____ 4. touch   d. able to spread easily

____ 5. pediatrician   e. not dirty

____ 6. clean   f. a doctor who treats children

Conversation with the Pediatrician

Practice the dialog with a partner.

What do you think this is?

It looks like conjunctivitis, or pink eye.

Yes. That's going around at preschool.

Here is a prescription for some antibiotic eye drops.

How often do I give them to my daughter?

Give them to her three times a day.

A Letter about Pink Eye

Read the letter from the preschool director. Then answer the questions.

> Dear Parents,
>   We have had several cases of conjunctivitis (pink eye) at our preschool. Conjunctivitis is a bacterial or viral infection of the eye. Your child may have conjunctivitis if the eye is red and has a yellow discharge. Please see your pediatrician immediately. Children with conjunctivitis cannot go to school. A child with bacterial conjunctivitis can return to school 24 hours after receiving antibiotic eye drops. A child with viral conjunctivitis needs to stay home until the symptoms disappear.

1. What is conjunctivitis? _____

2. Who do you need to see immediately? _____

3. When can a child with bacterial conjunctivitis return to school?

_____

4. How long does a child with viral conjunctivitis need to stay home?

_____

Sequence the pictures.

Listen. Then number the pictures in the correct order.

a. ____

c. ____

b. ____

d. ____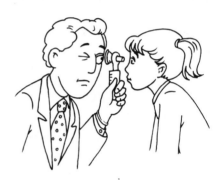

Problem Solving

I don't want to spread conjunctivitis. Put a check next to the good ideas.
Write other good ideas on the lines below.

____ disinfect doorknobs and counters

____ wash hands with warm water and soap

____ touch my face with hands

____ go to a swimming pool

____ throw away old eye makeup

____ change my pillowcase

____ share wash cloths and towels

____ use antibiotic eye drops

____ go to school with a red eye

____ see a doctor

_____

_____

What about you?

Check *Yes* or *No*. Then write the questions and ask your partner.

Yes   No

___ ___ 1. I sometimes have conjunctivitis.

<u>Do you sometimes have conjunctivitis?</u>

___ ___ 2. I make a doctor's appointment when I have an infection.

_____

___ ___ 3. I go places when I have an infection.

_____

___ ___ 4. I get prescriptions from a doctor for medication.

_____

___ ___ 5. I always try to keep my hands clean.

_____

Topics for Discussion or Writing

1. For what other reasons can you have red and itchy eyes?

2. What other infections or diseases are contagious?

3. Do you get infections? If so, what do you do to stop them from spreading?

I want to translate for her now.

LESSON 13

Translating at the Doctor's Office

Mi-Ok has **arthritis.** It affects her hands. It is difficult for her to cook. It hurts to slice vegetables. It hurts to pick up pots. She can't open jars. Her son, Young-Jae, takes her to the doctor.

Mi-Ok speaks Korean. The doctor speaks English. Young-Jae helps his mother and the doctor understand each other. Young-Jae tells the doctor about his mother's problems. The doctor examines Mi-Ok's hands for a long time.

The doctor talks about arthritis **medication.** Young-Jae translates the information for his mother. The doctor talks about other treatments: **injections, physical therapy,** and **surgery.** The doctor stops speaking often. Young-Jae explains everything in Korean. Mi-Ok nods her head. She understands the information.

The doctor writes a **prescription** for her. "These **pills** may help you," he says. "I know you need your hands for cooking. Good luck."

They leave the doctor's office. Young-Jae looks at his mother. "Let's try the medication, Mom. Maybe you can cook without **pain.**"

"I need time to think about this," says Mi-Ok. "Let's eat out tonight."

Check *Yes* or *No*.

Yes   No

____ ____ 1. Mi-Ok has arthritis.

____ ____ 2. It affects her knees.

____ ____ 3. It is difficult for her to cook.

____ ____ 4. She can open jars.

____ ____ 5. The doctor speaks Korean.

____ ____ 6. The doctor talks about arthritis medication.

____ ____ 7. Young-Jae translates the information for his mother.

____ ____ 8. The doctor writes a prescription for Mi-Ok.

____ ____ 9. The doctor gives her an injection.

____ ____ 10. Mi-Ok goes to the pharmacy for the medication.

Which category is it?

Chinese	hips	Korean	shoulders
English	injections	medication	Spanish
hands	knees	physical therapy	surgery

Languages	Arthritis Treatments	Body Parts that Arthritis Affects
1. _____	1. _____	1. _____
2. _____	2. _____	2. _____
3. _____	3. _____	3. _____
4. _____	4. _____	4. _____

Matching: Meanings

____ 1. pills   a. containers with lids for storing food

____ 2. injections   b. medical care

____ 3. arthritis   c. to change from one language to another

____ 4. treatment   d. shots of medicine from a syringe, or needle

____ 5. jars   e. small round tablets of medicine

____ 6. translate   f. a disease or condition that causes pain in
                          the joints

Conversation with a Doctor

Practice the dialog with a partner.

What do you think, Doctor?

Well, there are many treatments for arthritis.

What are they?

First, let's talk about medications. There are several drugs that may help.

Can you please wait a moment? I want to translate.

Yes. We want your mother to understand everything.

A Prescription for Arthritis Medication

Read Mi-Ok's prescription. Then answer the questions.

DOCTOR JOHN MILLER
WEST VILLAGE MEDICAL GROUP

Mi-Ok Park

Arthredux
Take one tablet daily

DOCTOR'S SIGNATURE _John Miller_

REFILLS: 3

1. What is the doctor's name? _____

2. What is Mi-Ok's last name? _____

3. How many tablets should she take daily? _____

4. How many refills does she have? _____

Listen. Check the correct picture.

1.

a. ____   b. ____

3.

a. ____   b. ____

2.

a. ____   b. ____

Problem Solving

My mother is going to the doctor. She speaks Korean. She doesn't understand English well. What can I do? Put a check next to the good ideas. Write other ideas on the lines below.

____ tell her to study English

____ hire a translator for her

____ go with her and translate

____ send a young child to help her

____ ask if the office has a translator

____ find medical information in Korean

____ find a doctor who speaks Korean

____ send her back to Korea for help

____ give the doctor a Korean dictionary

____ tell her it's OK to understand a little

_____   _____

What about you?

Check *Yes* or *No*. Then write the questions and ask your partner.

Yes   No

____ ____ 1. I think arthritis is a serious problem.

<u>**Do you think arthritis is a serious problem?**</u>

____ ____ 2. I help people in my family at doctor's appointments.

_____

____ ____ 3. I translate at doctor's appointments.

_____

____ ____ 4. I think it's important for a doctor and patient to understand each other.

_____

____ ____ 5. I think arthritis medication helps people.

_____

Topics for Discussion or Writing

1. In what ways do you use your hands in the kitchen?

2. What jobs are difficult if you have arthritis in your hands?

3. In what places is it important or useful for you to have a translator?

LESSON 14

A Bad Cut

Javier is a cook in a restaurant. Right now he is cutting an onion for some onion soup. He is using a very sharp knife. The knife slips and cuts his **index finger.** "Ouch!" says Javier. He drops the knife and looks at the **cut.** It is long and deep. It hurts a lot. Javier grabs a clean towel. He wraps it tightly around his finger.

Helen, the restaurant manager, runs over to Javier. "Are you okay?" she asks.

"No," says Javier. "This is a bad cut."

"Let me see it," says Helen.

"Not now," says Javier. "I need to apply **pressure.**" After 20 minutes, Javier and Helen look at the cut. It's still bleeding a lot.

"You need **stitches,**" says Helen.

Javier calls his sister. She drives him to an **emergency clinic.** The doctor gives Javier seven stitches. Then he gives him a **tetanus shot.** Javier's sister drives him home. He needs to take the rest of the day off. "Don't worry about dinner," says his sister. "I'll bring you some onion soup from the restaurant."

Check Yes **or** No.

Yes   No

_____ _____ 1. Javier is a restaurant manager.

_____ _____ 2. A knife slips and cuts Javier's index finger.

_____ _____ 3. The cut is long and deep.

_____ _____ 4. Javier wraps a dirty towel tightly around his finger.

_____ _____ 5. Javier applies pressure for 30 minutes.

_____ _____ 6. Helen tells Javier he needs stitches.

_____ _____ 7. Javier's sister drives him to an emergency clinic.

_____ _____ 8. The doctor gives Javier 17 stitches.

_____ _____ 9. The doctor gives him a tetanus shot.

_____ _____ 10. Javier needs to go back to the restaurant.

Complete each sentence.

applies	cuts	drops	grabs
calls	drives	gives	wraps

1. A knife slips and _____ Javier's index finger.

2. He _____ the knife and looks at the cut.

3. Javier _____ a clean towel.

4. He _____ it tightly around his finger.

5. Javier _____ pressure for 20 minutes.

6. Javier needs stitches. He _____ his sister.

7. His sister _____ him to an emergency clinic.

8. The doctor _____ him stitches and a tetanus shot.

Matching: Meanings

____ 1. pressure   a. losing blood from the body

____ 2. cut   b. the force from pushing on something

____ 3. tetanus   c. an injury from something sharp

____ 4. bleeding   d. a disease from an infection in a cut

____ 5. stitches   e. the finger next to the thumb

____ 6. index finger   f. medical sewing to close a bad cut

Conversation at the Emergency Clinic

Practice the dialog with a partner.

What happened?

I cut my finger badly.

When?

About a half hour ago.

Did you put anything on it?

No. Just a towel.

This is deep. You need stitches.

When was your last tetanus shot?

Maybe six or seven years ago.

You need another one today.

Caring for Stitches

Read the instructions that tell Javier how to care for his stitches. Then answer the questions.

> - Keep your stitches dry for the first 24 hours.
> - Put antibiotic ointment on your stitches twice a day.
> - Return to the clinic in five days.
> - Take a pain reliever if necessary.
> - Watch for signs of infection. Come in immediately if you notice any redness, drainage, warmth, or swelling.

1. For how long does Javier need to keep his stitches dry? _____

2. How often does he need to put on antibiotic ointment? _____

3. When does he need to return to the clinic? _____

4. What does he need to watch for? _____

Sequence the pictures.

Listen and number the pictures in the correct order.

a. ____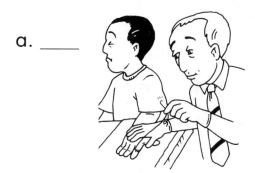

c. ____

b. ____

d. ____

Checklist

Here are things that can help a bad cut. Put a check next to the things you have at home. Write other things that can help on the lines below.

____ clean towel   ____ emergency clinic information

____ antibiotic ointment   ____ adhesive tape

____ bandages   ____ sterile gauze

____ tetanus shot   ____ antiseptic

____ tweezers   ____ needle and thread for surgical stitches

_____   _____

What about you?

Check *Yes* or *No*. Then write the questions and ask your partner.

Yes   No

____ ____ 1. I sometimes cut myself.

<u>Do you sometimes cut yourself?</u> _____

____ ____ 2. I have things to take care of a cut at home.

_____

____ ____ 3. I have things to take care of a cut at work.

_____

____ ____ 4. I have a person to call in an emergency.

_____

____ ____ 5. I know where I can get medical help in my area.

_____

Topics for Discussion or Writing

1. What kinds of injuries do people have where you work?

2. Where can you get medical help in your area? What is the nearest hospital or emergency clinic?

3. Who can you call when you need help? Why do you call this person?

Health Words

Lesson 1: Choosing Juice

chemical – material that is made up of an element or a compound

dye – something used to change colors

healthy – good for you

ingredients – the items that are part of a product

nutrition facts – information about what a food has in it

Lesson 2: Allergic to Shellfish

allergic – having or getting a physical reaction from eating, breathing, or touching something that makes you sick

breathing – taking air in and out of the lungs

food allergy – strong reaction from eating or drinking something

rash – red spots on the skin

upset stomach – a bad feeling or pain in the stomach

Lesson 3: Under Stress

exam – a close look by a doctor

headaches – pains in the head

stress – physical or mental pain caused by mental or emotional pressure

symptoms – signs of a physical problem

test – a medical process to find information about a person's condition

Lesson 4: A Heavy Box

back – the body part opposite the chest and stomach

hips – the joints between the waist and thighs

hurt – to cause pain or damage

joint – a part of the body where two or more bones come together

knees – the joints between the upper leg and lower leg

Lesson 5: A Shoulder Injury

injury – damage to a part of the body

painful – hurting, feeling bad

physical therapy – treatment of an injury using special exercises

shoulder – body part between the neck and upper arm

surgery – operation on the body

Lesson 6: Flossing Helps

bacteria – germs

decay – a process of becoming destroyed or in a bad condition

dental floss – special thread for removing food and plaque between teeth

dentist – doctor for teeth

diet – the food you eat

floss – to clean between teeth with a special thread

fluoride – a substance that helps prevent tooth decay

gum – the part of the mouth that holds the teeth

plaque – film on teeth where bacteria can grow

teeth – hard, white objects in the mouth for biting and chewing

Lesson 7: Two Cutting Boards

bacteria – germs

chlorine bleach – a chemical for cleaning

hand – body part at the end of each arm

raw – not cooked

Lesson 8: Getting a Refill

asthma – a medical condition that makes it hard to breathe

breathe – to take air into and out of the lungs

medication – another word for medicine; a drug; something you take if you are sick, to make you feel better

pharmacy – drugstore; a store or an area in a store where you buy medications

prescription – a doctor's order for medication

refill – another supply of the same medication

Lesson 9: Calling Poison Control

child-resistant – difficult for a child to open

poison – something that makes you very sick or kills you

vitamin – a pill with substances for good health

Lesson 10: Packing for the Hospital

allergic – having or getting a physical reaction from eating, breathing, or touching something that makes you sick

allergy – a physical reaction from eating, breathing, or touching something that makes you sick

antibiotics – strong drugs used to fight illness

chart – place to record medical information

health insurance – contract with a company that helps pay for medical care

hospital – place to get medical help when you are sick or injured

medication – another word for medicine; a drug; something you take if you are sick, to make you feel better

prescription drugs – medication you can get only with an order from a doctor

Lesson 11: Talking about Alcohol

alcohol – a beverage or drink that can make a person drunk

hearing – the sense that you use to listen

reactions – responses to something dangerous

vision – eyesight

Lesson 12: A Child with Pink Eye

antibiotic – having a strong drug used to fight bacterial illness

appointment – a specific day and time to see someone (such as a doctor)

bacterial – caused by a very small living thing that makes people sick

conjunctivitis – an infection in the eye; pink eye

contagious – able to spread easily from person to person, such as a disease

discharge – fluid that comes out of a body part

eye drops – liquid medication for the eyes

infection – a disease or illness

itchy – having an unpleasant feeling that you need to rub your skin or a body part

pediatrician – a doctor who treats children

viral – caused by a very small living thing that makes people sick, but different from the living thing that causes bacterial illnesses

Lesson 13: Translating at the Doctor's Office

arthritis – a disease or condition that causes pain in the joints

injection – a way to get medicine into the body, using a special needle

joints – parts of the body where two or more bones come together

medication – another word for medicine; a drug; something you take if you are sick, to make you feel better

pain – bad feeling when a part of the body hurts

physical therapy – treatment of a condition using special exercises

pills – small round tablets of medicine

prescription – a doctor's order for medication

surgery – an operation on the body

Lesson 14: A Bad Cut

cut – an injury from something sharp

emergency clinic – a place to go for medical help that you need right away

index finger – the finger next to the thumb

pressure – the force from pressing on something

shot – a way to get medication inside the body, using a special needle

stitches – medical sewing to close a cut

tetanus – a disease from an infection in a cut

Listening Exercise Prompts

Lesson 3

Sequence the pictures. (p. 20)

1. Salman worries about paying his bills.
2. He gets headaches, and his neck hurts.
3. Salman visits the doctor and has an exam.
4. Salman and his family go to a movie.

Lesson 4

Listen. Check the correct picture. (p. 26)

1. Bend at your hips and knees only.
2. Hold the box close to your body.
3. Take small steps.

Lesson 5

Sequence the pictures. (p. 32)

1. Julia slips on some ice.
2. She has shoulder surgery.
3. She uses weights and pulleys.
4. Julia wants to start swimming.

Lesson 8

Sequence the pictures. (p. 50)

1. Ted takes his medication every day.
2. He has no medication.
3. He calls the pharmacy.
4. He tells the pharmacy assistant his name.

Lesson 9

Sequence the pictures. (p. 56)

1. Kate gives Connor a vitamin.
2. She puts the vitamins on the counter and answers the telephone.
3. Connor picks up the open bottle and runs.
4. He is in his room chewing vitamins.

Lesson 11

Listen. Check the correct picture. (p. 68)

1. Alcohol affects a person's vision.
2. Alcohol causes accidents.
3. Tell your teenager to call any time.

Lesson 12

Sequence the pictures. (p. 74)

1. Rachel's left eye is very red and itchy.
2. Doctor Linzer examines Rachel's eye.
3. The doctor writes a prescription for some antibiotic eye drops.
4. Rachel needs to wash her hands with warm water and soap.

Lesson 13

Listen. Check the correct picture. (p. 80)

1. The arthritis affects her hands.
2. It hurts to pick up pots.
3. The doctor talks about injections.

Lesson 14

Sequence the pictures. (p. 86)

1. Javier cuts his index finger with a sharp knife.
2. Javier wraps a clean towel tightly around his finger.
3. His sister drives him to an emergency clinic.
4. The doctor gives him seven stitches.

Answer Key

Lesson 1
Check Yes or No. (p. 5)
1. yes
2. no
3. no
4. yes
5. yes
6. no
7. yes
8. no
9. yes
10. no

Complete each sentence. (p. 6)
1. supermarket
2. bottle
3. label
4. juice
5. chemicals
6. dye
7. family
8. shopping cart

Matching: Opposites (p. 6)
1. d
2. f
3. c
4. b
5. a
6. e

Nutrition Facts Label (p. 7)
1. Sunshine Orange Juice Drink
2. water
3. sodium benzoate
4. Yellow #5 dye
5. 10%

How much juice is there? (p. 8)
1. 100%
2. 10%

Lesson 2
Check Yes or No. (p. 11)
1. yes
2. no
3. no
4. yes
5. yes
6. yes
7. no
8. no
9. yes
10. no

Which category is it? (p. 12)
Signs of Allergic Reaction
1. rash
2. upset stomach
3. swelling
4. breathing problems

Things in the Kitchen
1. utensils
2. counter
3. grill
4. cutting board

Shellfish
1. lobster
2. clams
3. crab
4. shrimp

Matching: Opposites (p. 12)
1. f
2. d
3. e
4. a
5. b
6. c

Allergic Reactions to Food (p. 13)
1. 911
2. if breathing is difficult
3. epinephrine or emergency medicine
4. medication
5. if a person stops breathing

Match the words and pictures. (p. 14)
1. seafood 2. shellfish 3. fish

Checklist (p. 14)
Check: halibut, swordfish, salmon, tuna, trout, cod, bass

Lesson 3
Check Yes or No. (p. 17)
1. no
2. no
3. yes
4. yes
5. no
6. yes
7. yes
8. no
9. no
10. yes

Complete each sentence. (p. 18)
1. works
2. supports
3. worries
4. gets
5. grinds
6. visits
7. talks
8. says

Matching: Meanings (p. 18)
1. d
2. c
3. b
4. f
5. a
6. e

Problems with Stress (p. 19)
1. worrying about many things, such as job, money, family, illness, retirement, or the death of a family member; working a lot
2. your health
3. insomnia, backaches, headaches
4. high blood pressure, heart disease

Sequence the pictures. (p. 20)
a. 2
b. 3
c. 4
d. 1

Lesson 4
Check Yes or No. (p. 23)
1. yes
2. no
3. yes
4. yes
5. yes
6. no
7. no
8. yes
9. no
10. no

Complete each sentence. (p. 24)
1. boxes
2. floor
3. legs
4. supervisor
5. knees
6. body
7. steps
8. help

Matching: Opposites (p. 24)

1. c   3. f   5. b
2. e   4. a   6. d

Lifting a Heavy Box (p. 25)

Learners should circle picture 2 and picture 3.

Listen. Check the correct picture. (p. 26)

1. a   2. a   3. b

Lesson 5

Check *Yes* or *No*. (p. 29)

1. no	4. no	7. yes	9. no
2. yes	5. yes	8. no	10. no
3. yes	6. yes		

Which category is it? (p. 30)

Things that Help Julia

1. weights   3. exercise
2. rest   4. therapy

People who Help Julia

1. physical therapist
2. surgeon
3. husband
4. doctor

Places to Slip

1. steps   3. bathtub
2. patio   4. floor

Matching: Meanings (p. 30)

1. c   3. d   5. a
2. e   4. f   6. b

Getting Physical Therapy (p. 31)

1. post-surgery care, joint and muscle pain, sports and work injuries
2. 5671 Lakeshore Drive
3. 714-555-9348
4. Monday-Friday 7:00 AM to 6:00 PM

Sequence the pictures. (p. 32)

a. 4   b. 1   c. 2   d. 3

Lesson 6

Check Yes or No. (p. 35)

1. yes	4. no	7. no	9. yes
2. no	5. yes	8. no	10. yes
3. no	6. yes		

Which category is it? (p. 36)

Things that Help Teeth

1. toothbrush   3. toothpaste
2. dental floss   4. dental exam

Dental Problems

1. gum disease   3. decay
2. plaque   4. cavities

Food and Drinks to Avoid

1. sugar   3. candy
2. soda   4. sweetened juice

Matching: Meanings (p. 36)

1. b   3. a   5. d
2. e   4. f   6. c

Using Dental Floss (p. 37)

1. 18 inches (45 cm)
2. around his middle fingers
3. between his teeth and along the gumline
4. to a clean section
5. one or more times a day

Match the words and pictures. (p. 38)

1. fluoride toothpaste
2. dental floss
3. dental exam

Lesson 7

Check *Yes* or *No*. (p. 41)

1. no	4. yes	7. yes	9. no
2. yes	5. yes	8. yes	10. yes
3. no	6. no		

Complete each sentence. (p. 42)

1. soapy   5. different
2. plastic   6. hot
3. small   7. chlorine
4. raw   8. kitchen

Matching: Meanings (p. 42)

1. c   3. b   5. d
2. e   4. a

Cleaning a Cutting Board (p. 43)

1. hot, soapy water
2. one teaspoon of chlorine bleach in one quart of water
3. after using it for raw foods
4. two

Label the items. (p. 44)

1. towel
2. counter
3. knife
4. cutting board
5. chicken
6. vegetables

Lesson 8

Check *Yes* or *No*. (p. 47)

1. yes
2. yes
3. no
4. yes
5. yes
6. no
7. no
8. no
9. yes
10. no

Which category is it? (p. 48)

Information on Medicine Packages

1. doctor's name
2. patient's name
3. prescription number
4. pharmacy phone number

Causes of Breathing Problems

1. asthma
2. smoking
3. allergies
4. lung diseases

Things in a Medicine Cabinet

1. eye drops
2. aspirin
3. medication
4. thermometer

Matching: Meanings (p. 48)

1. d
2. c
3. f
4. a
5. e
6. b

A Medication Label (p. 49)

1. 1091164
2. Gloria Taylor, MD
3. 2650 L Street
4. Ted Chu
5. none

Sequence the pictures. (p. 50)

a. 3
b. 4
c. 2
d. 1

Lesson 9

Check *Yes* or *No*. (p. 53)

1. yes
2. yes
3. no
4. yes
5. yes
6. no
7. no
8. yes
9. no
10. yes

Complete each sentence. (p. 54)

1. gives
2. rings
3. forgets
4. puts
5. picks up
6. hangs up
7. thinks
8. runs

Matching: Meanings (p. 54)

1. e
2. a
3. b
4. f
5. d
6. c

Directions for Taking Vitamins (p. 55)

1. one
2. out of reach of children
3. a doctor or poison control center
4. if the safety seal is torn or missing

Sequence the pictures. (p. 56)

a. 3
b. 4
c. 1
d. 2

Lesson 10

Check *Yes* or *No*. (p. 59)

1. no
2. yes
3. yes
4. yes
5. no
6. no
7. no
8. yes
9. yes
10. no

Which category is it? (p. 60)

Hospital Staff

1. nurse
2. dietician
3. social worker
4. doctor

Personal Items

1. razor
2. shampoo
3. toothbrush
4. toothpaste

Clothing for the Hospital

1. pajamas
2. slippers
3. nightgown
4. bathrobe

Matching: Meanings (p. 60)

1. d
2. a
3. b
4. f
5. c
6. e

An Insurance Card (p. 61)

1. Rolf Schmidt
2. Green Cross HMO
3. Dong Hieu
4. (619) 555-6720

Label the items. (p. 62)

1. razor
2. toothpaste
3. toothbrush
4. list of allergies
5. prescription drugs
6. bathrobe
7. pajamas
8. slippers
9. suitcase

Lesson 11
Check *Yes* or *No*. (p. 65)
1. no 4. no 7. no 9. yes
2. yes 5. yes 8. no 10. no
3. yes 6. yes

Complete each sentence. (p. 66)
1. teenager 5. passenger
2. alcohol 6. friends
3. vision 7. money
4. accidents 8. questions

Matching: Opposites (p. 66)
1. b 3. e 5. f
2. a 4. d 6. c

Teenagers and Alcohol (p. 67)
1. teenagers 3. 50%
2. alcohol 4. binge drink

Listen. Check the correct picture. (p. 68)
1. a 2. b 3. b

Lesson 12
Check *Yes* or *No*. (p. 71)
1. yes 4. yes 7. yes 9. yes
2. yes 5. no 8. no 10. yes
3. no 6. no

Complete each sentence. (p. 72)
1. eye 5. discharge
2. preschool 6. infection
3. conjunctivitis 7. eye drops
4. pediatrician 8. hands

Matching: Meanings (p. 72)
1. d 3. a 5. f
2. c 4. b 6. e

A Letter about Pink Eye (p. 73)
1. a bacterial or viral infection of the eye
2. your pediatrician
3. 24 hours after receiving antibiotic eye drops
4. until the symptoms disappear

Sequence the pictures. (p. 74)
a. 3 b. 4 c. 1 d. 2

Lesson 13
Check *Yes* or *No*. (p. 77)
1. yes 4. no 7. yes 9. no
2. no 5. no 8. yes 10. no
3. yes 6. yes

Which category is it? (p. 78)
Languages
1. Spanish 3. Korean
2. Chinese 4. English

Arthritis Treatments
1. physical therapy 3. surgery
2. injections 4. medication

Body Parts Arthritis Affects
1. hands 3. shoulders
2. knees 4. hips

Matching: Meanings (p. 78)
1. e 3. f 5. a
2. d 4. b 6. c

A Prescription for Arthritis Medication (p. 79)
1. John Miller 3. one
2. Park 4. three

Listen. Check the correct picture. (p. 80)
1. a 2. a 3. b

Lesson 14
Check *Yes* or *No*. (p. 83)
1. no 4. no 7. yes 9. yes
2. yes 5. no 8. no 10. no
3. yes 6. yes

Complete each sentence. (p. 84)
1. cuts 5. applies
2. drops 6. calls
3. grabs 7. drives
4. wraps 8. gives

Matching: Meanings (p. 84)
1. b 3. d 5. f
2. c 4. a 6. e

Caring for Stitches (p. 85)
1. 24 hours
2. twice a day
3. in five days
4. signs of infection; redness, drainage, warmth, swelling

Sequence the pictures. (p. 86)
a. 4 b. 2 c. 1 d. 3